D1322555

I Am With You Always

Living with Loneliness

Siobhán O'Keeffe SHJM

ISBN: 978 1 78812 026 5

Designed by Messenger Publications Design Department
Typeset in Times New Roman and Charlemagne Std
Printed by Nicholson & Bass Ltd

Messenger Publications,
37 Lower Leeson Street, Dublin 2
www.messenger.ie

CONTENTS

DEDICATION
Dedicated to each Sister of the Sacred Hearts of Jesus and Mary.

INTRODUCTION

We stand and gaze at the beauty of a rainbow, bowing down to worship God. A rainbow is one of nature's great beauties. Its colours and hues come together to form a magnificent whole, a symbol of our lives.

The human person is made for spiritual, emotional and social connection with others. When this does not happen many suffer from feelings of isolation and separation that leave them deeply lonely. This sense of isolation can have a profoundly negative effect on their spiritual, emotional and physical health which, if not addressed, can lead to depression and other illnesses. Each life is made up of periods of joy and sorrow, happiness and sadness, belonging and loneliness.

Fully human and fully divine, Jesus was no stranger to loneliness both during his active ministry, when his message was not understood and people did not recognise who he was, 'Have I been with you all this time, Philip, said Jesus to him, and you still do not know me?' (Jn 14:9), and as he endured the passion (Mt 27:47). His mother Mary must have experienced a profound feeling of loneliness as she came to terms with her miraculous pregnancy, 'She was deeply disturbed by these words and asked herself what this greeting could mean' (Lk 1:30) and again at the foot of the cross as she witnessed her beloved Son die. 'Near the cross of Jesus stood his mother' (Jn 19:25).

You may have picked up this little book because you or your friend are struggling with a very human loneliness and you need some comfort and support at this time. I wish to reassure you that you are not alone on your journey as loneliness is experienced by most people at some time in their lives. We are created for union with God, others and ourselves, however, on occasion we can feel fragmented and alone, struggling to maintain our own inner peace because we are lonely.

People of all ages suffer from loneliness. A mother grieves when she leaves her child in the classroom on the child's first day in school and teachers are left consoling the little one as she walks away. Two or three hours is an eternity in this little persons' life until they are re-united with mother at 'going home time'. Squeals of delight ring out when she appears at the classroom door. As life moves forward, the child who is bullied in school, the employee who struggles in the workplace because they feel that they do not fit in and the CEO who is challenged with making difficult decisions all experience loneliness in different ways.

Aloneness and *loneliness* are very different – we may be all alone and very much at peace. Loneliness is a feeling of disconnection or incompleteness caused by a lack of human connection for various reasons; bereavement, unemployment, illness, disability, being housebound, facing a terminal illness or death, living as a refugee, asylum seeker or trafficked person. Whatever the source of our pain, it is important that we feel able to name for ourselves and also to another the anguish of soul that we are experiencing. Naming our pain can help to loosen its tight grip on our hearts and begin to set us free from its negative control. Children will need guidance and support to tell someone how they are feeling as all too often they suffer in silence as they have not learned strategies for dealing with this human emotion. Loneliness that is not acknowledged or worked through is at risk of deepening and may lead to more serious emotional or spiritual problems.

Experiencing a period of loneliness in our lives is painful but it does not have to be totally negative. We may learn more about ourselves and the importance of positive relationships in our lives. We are offered an opportunity to give thanks for all who have blessed us and to seek reconciliation if this is necessary. We realise that 'no man is an island' and that we all need each other for good quality of life. We examine our expectations of ourselves or others and realise that no one can completely fill that deep inner space in our hearts that God has reserved for himself alone. We echo the prayer of St Augustine when he prays, 'You have made us for yourself, and our hearts are restless, until they can find rest in you'. This helps us to deepen our life of prayer and many words of hope are offered to us in Scripture, 'if God is for us, who can be against us?' (Rom 8:31) or 'I will give you another advocate to be with you forever' (Jn 14:16).

As we grow through our experience, we are encouraged to reach out to others and to be a good friend to members of our family, community and workplace. We reflect on the loneliness that pervades our society and are encouraged to join organisations that befriend others and add quality of life to people who may be at risk of isolation through no fault of their own. Often much positive care is offered by people who themselves have lived through and come through difficult times – they have some insight into the loneliness that you may be feeling and wish to support you on your journey –

these wounded healers have been graced with the ointment of understanding and wish to empathise with you on your journey. They will not judge or criticise you for what you are feeling but through their compassion will help you to keep a perspective on your experience and help you to move forward to a brighter tomorrow. They offer you hope.

One of the great gifts that we may offer someone who is lonely is listening in the following ways:

- ❖ You come quietly into my world and let me be me.
- ❖ You respect my dignity, confidentiality and privacy.
- ❖ You try to understand me even if I am not making much sense.
- ❖ You attempt to grasp my point of view even if it is against you own convictions.
- ❖ You do not judge or criticise me for what I am feeling or may be unable to express.
- ❖ You acknowledge that deep listening to the pain in my heart at this time has left you somewhat drained but that this is ok.
- ❖ You do not tell me what I should do but allow me to discover solutions to my situations from deep within the clay of my soul.
- ❖ You accept my gratitude when I acknowledge that I appreciate your support and understanding.
- ❖ If I ask for a list of resources, scripture passages or other aids to my situation you do what you can to help me source these aids.
- ❖ You help me to realise that God has a good plan for my life, 'I know the plans I have in mind for you – it is Yahweh who speaks – plans for peace, not disaster, reserving a future full of hope for you' (Jer 29:11–13).

❖ You encourage me to take positive action to deal with the challenges that I face.

❖ Your compassionate attitude helps to restore my confidence and empowers me to move forward with my life richer for the experience that I have lived through.

There are also ways we can pursue self-help:

❖ Have a positive attitude to life.

❖ Smile, this helps to lighten mood and draws other people to a person.

❖ Acknowledge feelings and reach out for help.

❖ Keep a journal to record feelings in a safe place. Do not edit what is written, express raw feelings in their nakedness. There is no need to share this with anyone. When you feel better you can look back on how far you have come on your journey.

❖ Draw or paint feelings.

❖ Pray and ask for the guidance of the Holy Spirit to cope and move forward.

❖ Confide in a close friend.

❖ Be a friend to another.

❖ Stay in touch with friends and meet in person as much as possible. Do not become dependent on social media as this does not replace human contact.

❖ Eat a balanced diet.

❖ Seek medical help for any underlying conditions that may impact on mood.

❖ If able to leave home, go for a walk. Fresh air and exercise release mood enhancing chemicals in the body and help one to feel better.

❖ Join a relaxation or swimming class.

- ❖ Mindfulness, Yoga or meditation may be helpful.
- ❖ Develop an existing hobby or start a new one.
- ❖ Join a club that is of interest to you.
- ❖ Volunteer at a charity that needs volunteers.
- ❖ Read positive literature.
- ❖ Join the library. Libraries have lists of local activities that may be of interest and offer opportunities for people to make new friends.
- ❖ Expect to be accepted into new groups.
- ❖ Let go of painful memories of rejection and seek out any necessary help to do this.
- ❖ Pray – the Scriptures offer many words of encouragement, especially in the Psalms. Trust God, trust oneself, trust others.
- ❖ The Sacrament of Reconciliation offers healing and hope.
- ❖ Join a Justice and Peace group.
- ❖ Sign online petitions that support justice and peace issues.
- ❖ Speak to your line manager at work if loneliness is impacting on work performance. Support may be available to you through the Occupational Health Department of the organisation.
- ❖ Stay in close contact with your child's school ensuring that any issues are addressed earlier rather than later.
- ❖ Believe that this feeling of loneliness will pass.
- ❖ If it does not, seek professional help from your GP, counsellor or a member of the clergy.
- ❖ Prepare for retirement in good time – begin remote preparation early including financial planning.

In the following series of reflections I wish to invite you, dear reader, to enter into the experience of a wide range of people. I want you to 'taste' their loneliness so that you can develop an appreciation of the impact that loneliness has on their lives and of the role the Word of God and compassionate care can play in them coming through their valley of suffering to grow in intimacy with God, self and others.

I have attempted to look at this issue in such a way that a cross-section of spiritual and social contexts are considered. My aim is to encourage all sections of society to reach out in compassion to one another in order to help relieve this human suffering. In so doing, we will grow closer to God and each other.

Each reflection opens with a scriptural reference as the Word of God offers comfort, light and hope to us on our journey. Each reflection concludes with a 'thought to take away' on how that reflection may be lived out in today's world.

The excellent ministry offered by some voluntary and statutory organisations to support people at difficult times in their lives is highlighted. Appendices for extra advice and support are included.

May each person be consoled and strengthened to live through and beyond their loneliness into a joyful new day.

REFLECTION 1: THE LONELINESS OF JESUS

As Jesus was about to go up to Jerusalem, he took the twelve disciples aside by themselves, and said to them on the way 'Behold, we are going up to Jerusalem, and the Son of Man will be handed over to the chief priests and scribes, and they will condemn him to death; then they will hand him over to the Gentiles to be mocked and scourged and flogged and crucified; and on the third day He will be raised.' (Mt 20:17–19)

Here we are offered one of the deepest insights into the loneliness of Jesus as he prepared for his death. He took his closest friends aside to share with them the most heart-breaking news that they could possibly hear and to prepare them for what was about to happen. He who had journeyed with them over the previous three years was about to be betrayed and put to death.

In his humanity he needed them to know the reality of what was about to take place and to seek their companionship and support on this most awful journey. His heart was crushed and sore that his message of love had been so rejected and that the transformative power of his presence amongst them had made no life-giving difference in the lives of the scribes, Pharisees or Gentiles. I cannot possibly imagine the overwhelming sense of rejection and misunderstanding that he must have felt when his message of love was rejected and those whom he had helped and healed were now about to condemn him to a death. However, true to his mission, he tells his closest friends that he will proceeded to Calvary for the salvation of the world.

The loneliness of his closest friends at the impending death of their beloved master must have been too awful for words. As faithful friends they accompanied Jesus to Jerusalem. By his faithfulness to his mission, Jesus has left us a message of hope that he is with us always and that we can find life beyond loneliness when we place our trust in him and call on the love and support of our most faithful friends. Jesus rose beyond death and offered new life to the world.

THOUGHT TO TAKE AWAY

We too are offered new life beyond the most crushing loneliness when we place our hand deep into the hand of the crucified and risen Lord that we may too may be raised up.

REFLECTION 2: NOT MY WILL BUT THINE BE DONE

And going a little further, he threw himself on the ground and prayed. 'My Father, if it is possible, let this cup pass from Me; yet not as I want, but what you want.' (Mt 26:39)

Overcome with exhaustion, the loneliness of the journey has sapped all of Jesus' strength and courage to keep going. He is completely alone and feels that he cannot continue; his life blood is draining away; he has been betrayed, cast aside and rejected by most of humanity. He has suffered the most awful physical and emotional torture. He can see no way forward and cries out to his Father to rescue him from the ignominy of the cross. This must be one of the most heartfelt cries of anguish or loneliness that must ever have been heard on the face of the earth; it will have gone right to the heart of God. However, Jesus acknowledges his son-ship and wishes to up-hold the mission of the Father for the salvation of the world. He surrenders his own will to the will of the father and in this he finds the courage to go on, to complete the salvation story and to win true peace for himself and all humankind.

In this he has left us an example to follow – when our wills are in union with the will of the Father, we too receive the grace to live through any loneliness and to come to a new and deeper peace at the core of our souls.

THOUGHT TO TAKE AWAY

What is the loneliness that you may need to surrender to God today so that you may know the peace that Christ wishes to offer to you today?

REFLECTION 3: MARY, MOTHER OF GOD

Meanwhile, standing near the cross of Jesus were his mother and his mother's sister, Mary the wife of Clophas and Mary Magdalene. When Jesus saw his mother and the disciple whom he loved standing beside her, he said to his mother, 'Woman, here is your son'. Then he said to the disciple, 'Here is your mother'. And from that hour the disciple took her into his home. (Jn 19:25–28)

At the hour of Jesus' greatest anguish and need he reached out to comfort his mother Mary. She who had consented to the will of God and brought him into the world is now bereft at the anguish of her son. His precious life is slipping away before her – her grief knows no bounds. Consumed by her pain, and compassionate to the last, Jesus reaches into the depths of her loneliness and offers her words of comfort. He entrusts her to the care of his beloved disciple so that she would not be on her own and would be cared for all her days. Conscious of the needs of his beloved disciple, he entrusts him to the care of his beloved mother. They would share their lives as they journeyed ever closer to God. This act of great love relieved the loneliness of Mary and John and served as consolation to Mary, wife of Clophas and Mary Magdalene.

THOUGHT TO TAKE AWAY
At the time of our greatest loneliness, may we be filled with God's spirit that we may be able to reach out and respond to the needs of others.

REFLECTION 4: AN EMMAUS WALK

Now on the same day two of them were going to a village called Emmaus, about seven miles from Jerusalem, and talking with each other about all these things that had happened. While they were talking and discussing, Jesus himself came near and went with them, but their eyes were kept from recognising him. And he said to them, 'What are you discussing with each other while you walk along?' They stood still, looking sad. (Lk 24:13–18)

Jesus, their beloved Lord and master, has been crucified and put to death. These heartbroken men cannot comprehend the incomprehensible; they seek consolation in their shared friendship and go for a walk; they feel that walking and talking to each other may help to clear their heads and relieve the heartbreak that is tearing them apart. They are convinced that only those who knew him really well would understand what he had meant to them and how awful life without him is now. To crown it all, women had seen angels who said he was alive!

These things just do not happen and then a stranger appears amongst who seems to know 'nothing about these things'. At this point, these disciples are beginning to questioning their own sanity, what is going on and how will they cope? Jesus steps into the darkness of their despair 'but their eyes are kept from recognising him' (Lk 24:16).

They share their tale of woe with the stranger and offer him hospitality; after all that is what Jesus would have wanted them to do. Oh so suddenly, everything changes! Ever true to his mission, Jesus does not want them to remain sad, lost or without hope and reveals his true identity to them. Overcome with joy, they continue on their shared journey to bring the good news of his resurrection to all people.

At times of my greatest loss, the eyes of my hearts have sometimes been blinded by sadness and loneliness leaving me unable to recognise Jesus. Sometimes, during these times I have walked and talked with my closest friend and been helped to see a way through the anguish that I have felt. Through the compassion of my friend, I have come to a deeper understanding and appreciation of the compassion that Jesus himself has for me and all at our time of greatest need.

THOUGHT TO TAKE AWAY

What is the sadness or loss that you feel today that you need to share with your friends and Jesus himself?

REFLECTION 5:
COMPASSION, REDEMPTION AND MISSION

Jesus said to her, 'Everyone who drinks of this water will be thirsty again, but those who drink of the water that I will give will never be thirsty. The water that I will give will become in them a spring of water gushing up to eternal life.' The woman said to him, 'Sir give me this water, so that I may never be thirsty or have to keep coming here to draw water'. Jesus said to her, 'Go and call your husband and come back.' The woman answered him, 'I have no husband.' Jesus said to her, 'You are right in saying, "I have no husband" for you have had five husbands, and the one you have now is not your husband.' (Jn 4:13–18)

We are invited into the loneliness and inner hunger of a lady whose name we do not know and whose life is transformed when she meets Jesus. This woman has looked for fulfilment in many different places, not found it and is at a loss as to a way forward. The inner bucket of her soul has been drained by a number of broken relationships that have left her disillusioned, lonely and fearful of trusting again. Her embarrassment and sense of shame have led her to the well at a time when she knew that others would not be there, the last person that she expects to meet is Jesus. What a meeting that was! Jewish people did not relate to Samaritans but deeper gifts than a breakdown of prejudice are in store for she who had suffered so much.

Jesus wastes no time in asking her what she wants. He

reaches into her loneliness and transforms it when she honestly admits her reality to herself and to him. She no longer lives in shame but in liberation and goes forwards in mission to all of God's people. She does not need to go to the well early in the morning but can hold her head high, alive with a new joy because her heart has been healed – set free. The drought of her loneliness has been transformed into a well of joy. One of the gifts that she offers us rests in our acknowledgement of our deepest need to Jesus. When we honestly share with him the loneliness, sadness, grief or pain that rests deep in our hearts, he is able to transform it and send us forth on mission to all of Gods people. Like the woman, we have to recognise, own and acknowledge our need so that he can heal and free us.

THOUGHT TO TAKE AWAY

Jesus wishes to fill your bucket and send you forward on mission with renewed joy.

REFLECTION 6:
VICTIMS OF CHILDHOOD BULLYING

There are six things that the Lord hates,
seven that are an abomination to him;
haughty eyes, a lying tongue,
and hands that shed innocent blood,
a heart that devises wicked plans,
feet that hurry to run to evil,
a lying witness who testifies falsely,
and one who sows discord in a family.
(Prov 6:16–19)

In this reflection, we enter into the experience of Joe, a fourteen-year-old boy who is being bullied at school. He is just one of the many children who suffer bullying and the impact that it is having upon him, if not addressed, may endanger his life. Joe is just one of the many children who cry out to us for love and support when they fear the onslaught of the bully.

Bullying is an act of cowardice carried out by people who themselves are insecure and lacking in good personal relationship skills and can affect people of all ages, social classes and traditions. Traditionally, the bully targeted the vulnerability of their victim in the school playground or on the school bus. They diminished their self-esteem by name-calling, social exclusion or physical aggression. Today, the victim may be targeted because of race, colour, gender or sexual orientation. This may be done in person or through social media.

Joe says that he is being targeted because he consistently achieves the highest grades in all school subjects, is socially popular and excels on the sports field. He has a wide circle of friends, however, as soon as he opens his social media account, a barrage of abuse awaits him. He is reluctant to speak to his parents or teachers as they all feel that he is doing very well in school and he does not wish to worry them. When speaking to me in private, he has told me that he has never before felt more vulnerable. He weeps in private because he feels embarrassed and ashamed of his feelings of vulnerability and in his mind he hears, 'boys don't cry, man up, don't be a wimp'. He has told me that he feels that he is withdrawing from social relationships, not sleeping properly and is becoming depressed. He has been very frightened by the intensity of his feelings and has even considered suicide as he feels that no one understands his anguish. Isolation is becoming a hallmark of his experience; his loneliness is profound and maybe life-threatening.

I know that Joe is not alone in this awful experience.

Children always had a special place in the heart of Jesus and he reminds us of what our attitude to them should be: 'Let the little children come to me, and do not stop them; for it is to such as these that the kingdom of God belongs. Truly I tell you, whoever does not receive the kingdom of God as a little child shall not enter it' (Lk 18:16–17). In this he offers a word of encouragement and reassurance to all children but especially to those who suffer. He offers a warning to all who do not relate with compassion to all children. He instructs the bully on how they are to behave; 'You shall not take vengeance or bear a grudge against any of your people, but you shall love your neighbour as yourself' (Lev 19:18).

Support is available for anyone who is at risk of acting as a bully if they have the courage and humility to seek help. With the correct support they can turn away from their destructive behaviours and learn to respect others. Young people who have received good support speak of how they learnt to respond appropriately to bullies and how they themselves have grown and matured through their experience of pain. They have grown in self-knowledge and self-confidence as their inner spirit has grown stronger. Some have joined buddy schemes where they now support other young people who are recovering from an experience of bullying. They wish to share a message of hope with others so that they may be 'filled with all the fullness of God' (Eph 3:19).

THOUGHT TO TAKE AWAY

What steps may you need to take to address bullying issues in your school, home or workplace? Do not be afraid, God is with you in this essential work.

REFLECTION 7: YOUNG CARERS

Let the little children come to me, and do not stop them; for it is to such as these that the kingdom of God belongs. Truly I tell you, whoever does not receive the kingdom as a little child will never enter it. (Lk 18:16–18)

In my ministry to young people with early onset dementia I have had the privilege of supporting young carers whose parents or siblings have become disabled with early onset dementia. Early onset dementia is a form of dementia that affects people under the age of sixty-five. It is an illness that is often missed as symptoms may be confused with other illnesses and go undiagnosed and unsupported for a long period of time.

The person affected loses capacity to communicate effectively or to undertake everyday tasks. This leaves them feeling very frustrated, isolated and lonely. It is a very traumatic experience for the whole family and can place huge strain on family relationships. Each family member is affected and often suffers in silence. They may not know where to turn for support or the support that is available may not be appropriate to the needs of young people. This devastating illness robs the young carer of their childhood or young adulthood. Many other young people also assume the role of young carer as a parent, brother or sister need varying levels of help or support because of a physical, mental or special needs disability.

For some, a caring role is a very positive experience as they appreciate the opportunity to support their loved one at a difficult time in their lives. They also value the positive life skills that they gain through this experience. However, some speak of the overwhelming responsibilities that are placed on their shoulders leaving them feeling frightened and alone. Overnight they have been forced to 'leave childhood behind' and to grow up fast'. Their caring role obliges them to offer practical, emotional and social support to their loved one.

Tasks and roles young carers may take responsibility for can vary because of:

❖ the nature of the illness, disability or addiction
❖ the level and frequency of need for care and support
❖ the structure of the family as a whole
❖ the family's level of contact with health and social services
❖ the ethnic or cultural background of the family.

The gift that they offer often reduces the need for the ill person to be admitted into residential care until much later in the illness. As each year goes by, some young carers say that their sense of loneliness and isolation increases as their parent is not able to offer them the advice, support and companionship that they so desperately need at this critical time in their lives. They are reluctant to disclose their situation or challenges to teachers or peers as they fear being misunderstood. They are anxious that their disclosure may lead to the removal their loved one from the family home so they struggle on. Increasing isolation leaves both carer and cared for at risk of depression or abuse. Physical and emotional exhaustion limits the young person's ability to concentrate on their study or their attendance at school is compromised by their caring role. This impacts on their ability to make friends amongst their peer group and may also lead to anger and resentment towards the person cared for.

The question, *'why me?'* is often an expression of the deep sense of loneliness that they feel. There are no easy answers to this question. Gentle presence and open listening can help the young person process their feelings at this difficult time. The family often experiences financial hardship as the earning ability of the parent has been affected. Illness and disability consume a high level of family income adding to the anxiety and sense of isolation that the young person experiences as they do not have the resources that they need to participate in normal young people activities.

The actions of all who support young carers echo the psalmist when they pray,

When the righteous cry for help, the Lord hears,
and rescues them from all their troubles.
The Lord is near to the broken hearted,
and saves the crushed in spirit. (Ps 34:17–19)

THOUGHT TO TAKE AWAY

Young Carers in your community may need your support. How can you help them?

REFLECTION 8: CARING FOR AGEING PARENTS

When Jesus saw his mother and the disciple whom he loved standing beside her, he said to his mother, 'Woman, here is your son.' Then he said to the disciple, 'here is your mother.' And from that hour the disciple took her into his home. (Jn 19:26–28))

In this scripture reference we see where Jesus reached out in compassion to his mother and entrusted her to the care of his beloved disciple. He foresaw that she would need loving support in the years ahead and chose John to share her journey.

As a daughter and former nursing home manager, I am aware of the many challenges families face when deciding how best to offer sensitive support to ageing parents. The structure of family life and of society has changed and is unlikely to return to the norms of previous times. A higher standard of living for many, but sadly not all, better health care and other factors have helped people to living longer, leaving people with decisions as to how to best care for frail, ageing parents.

I have experienced the anguish of this decision and have on many occasions sat with families when they have come on informal visits to our nursing homes and tried to make a decision for their beloved father or mother. They have told me of how they live many miles away from the family home and are unable to visit as often as they would like or offer the daily personal care or support that is needed. On occasion, they have also spoken of the breakdown in family communication and of how this complicates the decisions that they now face. Many have shed bitter tears as they struggled to make a compassionate, wise decision knowing that most people prefer to live out their final days in the comfort and security of their own home.

Speaking privately to the parents or sometimes in the presence of their children they acknowledge that the demands of modern living. They have said, 'it wasn't like this in our day, times were different' but I feel so alone and so lonely. They have shared with me the loss that they feel when they miss their children's companionship and the life and energy generated by grandchildren. Their children speak of the guilt that they experience as they feel that they are failing in their duty of care to those who have gifted them with life. Their sense of guilt, real or imagined, is compounded when they feel that they are not upholding God's law, 'honour your father and your mother' (Ex 20:12) and that their absence may suggest that they are not 'listening' to the father who gave them life or respecting their mother now that she has grown old. Each family member suffers from different forms of loneliness and need sensitive understanding and support as they try to come to terms with their individual situation.

As Church and society we wish to support our parents and elderly. It is helpful if Church, state and secular organisations work together to uphold the dignity and rights of all family members. Some churches have outreach programmes that support the elderly and other vulnerable groups. They do this by visiting and praying with people, bringing them Holy Communion or by offering a listening ear. Age UK and other voluntary organisations provide a range of practical help and social support that helps to reduce the sense of isolation that some people may experience. University Chaplaincy supports the work of Christian student unions when they organise visits to nursing and care home residents. The lives of both the elderly and the young are enriched through these encounters. The loneliness of the elderly is reduced; youth learn from the life experience and wisdom of their elderly friends.

The glory of youth is their strength,
but the beauty of the aged is their grey hair. (Prov 20:29)

THOUGHT TO TAKE AWAY

What actions are needed to help older people feel more included in their local church and community? What can be done in your area? How can you help?

REFLECTION 9: NEW MOTHERS

Nothing will be impossible with God. (Lk 1:36)

I am forty years old and my husband is forty-two. I gave birth six weeks ago. I had dreamt of holding my own baby for many years but sadly my husband and I experienced infertility problems. My grief and loneliness at my barrenness were overwhelming at times. I feared I would never conceive. My sisters and friends all had children and the sound of children's voices playing in the garden pierced my soul as this joy eluded me. 'Would I ever have my own child?' the cry that burst forth from my soul, morning, noon and evening. Oh so unexpectedly, it happened. I could barely contain my joy when I discovered that I was pregnant. My husband and I wept with gladness as God had smiled upon us and gifted us with new life.

I had a wonderful pregnancy and uncomplicated delivery. When baby Matthew was placed on my breast, I felt that my sense of womanhood was complete; I had never felt more whole. Now my husband has returned to work. I am at home all day with a small baby who needs constant attention. I am alone and sometimes don't know what to do. This little lad screams when he is hungry, tired, soiled or lonely. I never thought that new motherhood could be so exhausting. My friends visited in the early weeks but they too have busy lives. My mother died many years ago and relationships with my in-laws are strained as they have different views and expectations than my husband's and mine. We keep our distance.

The Health Visitor called. She is very nice but has a large

caseload of new mothers and their babies. She just said, 'You have a beautiful healthy baby, you will adjust. Take it gently, all will be well'. That did not help to relieve the sense of loneliness and anxiety that I feel. I wish people would understand what I am going through. I am frightened for the future. Will it always be like this or is there something more serious the matter with me? I know that I am at risk of post-natal depression. I suffered periods of depression in my teenage years and again after the death of my mother. I know I need help. I will speak to my husband; we have always been very honest with each other but there has not been much time or energy for deeper conversations since little Matthew was born. I know that he too is struggling; I see it in his eyes or hear it in the tone of his voice when he says that the baby is taking up all my time and he feels a little excluded. I have never wanted to hurt him but I only have so much energy and I know that he is well supported by his work colleagues and football teammates. We will go to our kind GP and ask him to check baby Matthew to ensure that all is well. Our GP is very understanding and knows my story. I trust that if I need extra support he will guide me to organisations that can help me. I will pray to the great women of Scripture and ask them to place their mantle of protection over our family. May we glorify God for the wonderful gift of life that He has bestowed upon our family. We will live to praise him.

THOUGHT TO TAKE AWAY

Young Carers in your community may need your support. How can you help them?

REFLECTION 10:
CHRONICALLY ILL AND DISABLED PEOPLE

One day Peter and John were going up to the temple at the hour of prayer, at three o' clock in the afternoon. And a man lame from birth was being carried in. People would lay him daily at the gate of the temple called the beautiful gate so that he could ask for alms from those entering the temple. (Acts 3:1–3)

Lord, I bring before you today the loneliness of a disabled man whom I saw sitting on a street one Sunday morning in one of the world's major university cities. A carpet of thick snow had lain on the ground for several weeks; temperatures were now slowly creeping up to zero. This son of yours was not much older than you were when you began your public ministry. He sat alone in his wheelchair as many people streamed out of morning Mass. Led by a famous Mens' and Boys' choir, they had spent the previous hour singing out your praises.

I approached him and asked him if he would like something to eat. 'Coffee please, from Dunkin Donuts' was his laboured reply. 'Anything to eat?' A gentle shake of his head indicated, 'not now'. Unfamiliar with the city, I set forth to honour his request. Unable to locate his favourite Dunkin Donuts I joined a very long queue in Starbucks and hoped that my new friend did not fear that I had forgotten him. In due course, I returned to offer him his coffee. He graciously stretched out his very weak hands to receive the cup and he raised it ever so slowly to his dry, cracked lips. A few moments later a gentle nod of his head and an attempt to raise a thumb indicated to me that he was now able to continue to enjoy his coffee unaided.

I smiled gently at him and set forth to reflect ever more deeply on this Eucharistic experience that I had just been privileged to share. I wondered what illness or trauma had befallen this man? How had he arrived on the side of the street? How long had he sat there; where did he live and how might he might get home later that day? Who cared for him or put him to bed at night? How did he cope with the inevitable loneliness that must surely fall on his heart as he sees the crowd walk by each day? What were the fears of those who had left the banquet of the Lord but felt unable to stop to greet this Son of God? I felt deeply humbled that I had been graced to meet this man, to stop a share his journey if just for a brief moment and to be blessed by him. I prayed that in many ways throughout his day that people would go by and place him in the pool of God's healing love.

Now in Jerusalem by the Sheep Gate there is a pool, called in Hebrew Bethzatha which has five porticos. In these lay many invalids, blind, lame, and paralysed. One man was there for who had been ill for thirty-eight years. When Jesus saw him lying there and knew that he had been there a long time, he said to him, 'Do you want to be made well?' The sick man answered him, 'Sir, I have no one to put me into the pool when the water is stirred up; and while I am making my way, someone else steps down ahead of me.' Jesus said to him, 'Stand up, take your mat and walk.' At once, the man was made well, and he took up his mat and began to walk. (Jn 5:2–9)

THOUGHT TO TAKE AWAY

Open our eyes Lord to see the gifts that lie before us in 'the most unexpected places'.

REFLECTION 11: TERMINAL ILLNESS

We do not live (to) for ourselves, and we do not die (to) for ourselves. If we live, we live (to) for the Lord, and if we die, we die (to) for the Lord; so then whether we live or whether we die, we are the Lord's. For to this end Christ died and lived again, so that he might be Lord of both the dead and the living. (Rom 14:7–10)

In my work as a nurse, many people have shared with me the deep sense of loneliness that they experience when faced with a terminal illness. This is an emotion felt by people of all age groups, nationalities and cultures. A diagnosis of a terminal illness has often come as a shock; on other occasions it has confirmed for the person a deep-down suspicion that they may not recover from the illness that has weighed upon them over recent weeks or months. The greatest loneliness of which they speak is of how their illness and dying will impact on those closest to them. There is often a great sadness at the prospect of leaving loved and the ill person may feel that they are taking the cross of their loved ones upon themselves. They also speak of their own unfulfilled dreams and aspirations; 'I will not be here to give my daughter away on her wedding day' or 'I will never see my grandchildren'.

Feelings of deep loneliness are often accompanied by feelings of anger, denial and depression and take time to work through and resolve. When a younger person is terminally ill, they may feel robbed of the life that is being snatched away from them – this feels grossly unfair and the person may need much prayer and loving support to begin to come to terms with the deeply painful reality before them.

Loneliness and sadness may also exist if there is unresolved conflict in personal relationships. Many people are very grateful to have time to be reconciled with those with whom there may have been a misunderstanding. At times they may need professional or pastoral help to do this. The resolution of these deeply important issues brings healing and peace to the people involved. Many who have struggled over a period of time are enabled to enter into a time of deep calm and may live out the last days of their lives in deep peace. As there time on earth draws to a close they may echo the prayer of Jesus when he said, 'I am leaving the world and going to the Father' (Jn 16:28).

THOUGHT TO TAKE AWAY

Are you able to speak about the loneliness that you may feel when you are very ill? What help do you need to relieve your sense of isolation and loneliness at this time?

REFLECTION 12: LIFE-PARTNERS

Then the LORD God said, 'It is not good that man should be alone; I will make him a helper as his partner'. (Gn 2:18)

Over the years, a number of my unmarried friends have shared with me their desire for life-long intimacy with a life-partner and how challenging it can be to do this in a post-modern world. They wish to share their deepest thoughts, feelings and emotions with another human being who will help them to grow to fullness of life (Jn 10:10). They too desire to call forth life in this very special person and some may hope that one day they will be united in mind and spirit in the sacrament of marriage.

In today's society, many people find it difficult to meet a life-partner with whom they can have this deep spiritual and emotional intimacy. They long for a person who shares their Christian values, who wishes to dedicate their lives to God in all aspects of their lives. Relationship norms continue to change. Online dating, dating agencies and social media forums are changing the ways in which people meet each other. As well as these changes, life in a secular world can make this search more difficult. It is not easy to meet a life partner who shares the same values and vision as oneself. People may wonder if they will ever meet the person they are seeking or has God abandoned them in their search. Loneliness can become the bedfellow of the seeker.

Into this darkness, the prayer of the psalmist pours a message of comfort and hope:

Why are you cast down, O my soul,
and why are you disquieted within me?
Hope in God; for I shall praise him,
my help and my God. (Ps 43:5)

In due course, and in God's time, the person may be directed to the marriage partner God has chosen for them. Their hearts have been prepared by their prayer and search – joy will replace the anguish of the night, Jesus will be present as he was at the wedding feast of Cana as the happy couple commit themselves to each other for all eternity (Jn 2:2). The new wine of rejoicing will flow on this new day.

For this reason a man shall leave his father and mother and be joined to his wife, and the two shall become one flesh. So they are no longer two but one flesh. Therefore what God has joined together, let not man separate. (Mk 10:6–9)

THOUGHT TO TAKE AWAY

We pray for all who search for a life-partner, for all who have lost their partner and for those who are separated or divorced.

REFLECTION 13: WIDOWS AND WIDOWERS

He who finds a wife finds a good thing, and obtains favours from the Lord. (Prov 18:22)

The widow who after years of loving marriage loses their life-partner experiences a sadness that only they know. A lady told me, that there are no words to describe the sadness that she has felt since her husband died. With tears in her eyes, she spoke of the joy that she had dreamt of as a young girl came to pass when her beloved proposed marriage to her. True to tradition, her beloved had gone down on one knee and uttered the words, 'come, my darling; my beautiful one, come and make your home with me'.

Her wedding day was the happiest of her life. She said that they had the most wonderful times together but they had also know their share of trials and tribulations but they supported each other through the dark days. Their love grew deeper and stronger each passing day. They prayed together with their children each day and shared the Word of God with their children as they knew that God's word was the source of all life. On occasion, they were able to be together in a comfortable silence knowing that the other understood their soul.

Now her husband has been taken from her and she is left bereft. Nothing can ease the sadness that she feels; cooking a meal for one brings no joy, in the early days of her loss she had to discipline herself to eat balanced meals. His fireside chair stands empty as long winter evenings stretch out before her. Tears fall gently on her pillow as she lies on her bed of pain. Children and grandchildren visit – she shares memories of the happiness and struggles that were the fabric of her relationship with grandad. Her children and grandchildren encourage to stay strong and to put her faith in God as she builds her life without her husband. Deep in her heart she believes that God in his mercy has a new mission for her and she commits herself to a life of prayer. She is most grateful for the kindness of her family, friends and neighbours who have supported her since her beloved went home to God.

The real widow left alone has set her hope on God and continues in supplications and prayers night and day.
(1 Tim 5:5)

THOUGHT TO TAKE AWAY
A visit to a widow or widower brings much joy – a blessing for both people.

REFLECTION 14: CHOOSING A CAREER

Like good stewards of the manifold, serve one another with whatever gift each of you has received. (1 P 4:10)

The Gospel invites us to use all our God given gifts and talents for the up-building of his kingdom. However, it can be very difficult to discern where one's true vocation or way of life rests. Each year, thousands of students reach a crossroad on their journey as they leave school or university. Armed with expensive degrees, weighed down sometimes by huge financial debts and uncertain employment opportunities, some speak of feelings of great anxiety, insecurity and loneliness. The camaraderie of university life is over and now they have to step up to the plate and 'get a job'.

As followers of Jesus, many are aware that it is important that they make good ethical choices when choosing a career as not all paths lead to God. Making good choices serve the common good and builds up society while giving the person greater self-confidence and appreciation of who they are. However, a person can become lonely and disheartened in their search if 'things are not falling into place' or if they feel that their friends or colleagues are more successful than they are. It is important that they do not become discouraged as God loves each one deeply and has given each one a talent to serve him and humankind. The patient, gentle support of parents and true friends can help the young person to believe in themselves and to trust that in God's time, all will be well and they will discover the path that God has marked out for them.

Their prayer will echo the words of the psalmist:
Here I am:
In the scroll of the book it stands written of me,
I delight to do your will. (Ps 40: 7–8)

THOUGHT TO TAKE AWAY

When our choices are made in response to God's call, they bear witness to the goodness of God.

REFLECTION 15: SEAFARERS

When evening came, his disciples went down to the lake, got into the boat and started (across) to cross the lake to Capernaum. It was now dark, and Jesus had not yet come to them. The lake became rough because a strong wind was blowing. When they had rowed about three or four miles, they saw Jesus walking on the lake and coming near the boat and they were terrified. But he said to them, 'It is I, do not be afraid'. Then they wanted to take him into the boat, and immediately the boat reached the land towards which they were going. (Jn 6:16–21)

The beauty of the ocean captured my soul as a young boy. The sound of waves crashing on the rocks and the stillness of the waters as the sun glistened upon it late in the evening confirmed my desire to be a seafarer. I had heard of Jesus calling fishermen to follow him so I left my home and family at sixteen years of age to follow a call that he had placed deep in my heart. In my youthful enthusiasm, I did not realise the magnitude of the voyage on which I was embarking or the crushing loneliness that I would endure when I was separated from my family and friends for very long periods of time.

I am not alone in this suffering. Tens of thousands of us who work on ships all across the world. Most of us come from poorer countries where employment opportunities are limited and social welfare systems do not exist. We come from many different cultures and speak many different languages. This is enriching but can also be very difficult as we do not always understand each other, tensions can arise and we can feel very isolated. We are aware that workers in most other jobs do not have to suffer long-term separation from their homes, families and culture for up to a year at a time. We miss out on 'normal family life'. We are not at home to hear our children's first words, walk them to school or support them on the football pitch sideline. When our ships arrive at port, they may only be docked for a few hours as the cargo is unloaded. This does not offer us an opportunity to settle in any one place for a period of time where we could make friends or participate in local church or social life. Our living and working conditions are often very poor. On occasion, we feel that we are a hidden workforce and that the contribution we make can be taken for granted.

Our sense of isolation and loneliness can be compounded when all sorts of temptations are placed in our way in the ports. It can be so easy to succumb to illicit sexual encounters, alcohol or drug consumption or other vice. We do not choose to follow these paths but when the ache in our heart for human companionship is so deep and not receiving a life-giving response, we are tempted to succumb to our vulnerability.

We are most grateful to the organisations that help us through the very difficult and lonely times that we endure when we are far from home. Chaplains offer Prayer Services and Sacraments in two hundred ports across the world. Volunteer ship visitors provide companionship, a listening ear and practical support. They also escort seafarers to hospital appointments or help us to log on to the internet in the social centres that are provided at the ports. Other organisations work to ensure that our human rights are upheld and that our employment conditions are in line with national and international employment law.

Acts of human kindness remind us that Jesus who calmed the sea is present with us and we are very grateful to him and those who care for our wellbeing each day.

THOUGHT TO TAKE AWAY

❖ What spiritual or practical support can you offer to Seafarers in your local community?

❖ What do national and international Governments and trade organisations need to do to enhance the quality of life of the unsung heroes who staff the ships of the world each day?

REFLECTION 16: FARMERS

Now when he had spent everything, a severe famine occurred in that country, and he began to be impoverished. So he went and hired himself out to one of the citizens of that country, and he sent him into his fields to feed swine. And he would have gladly filled his stomach with the pods that the swine were eating, and no one was giving anything to him. (Lk 15:14–16)

I know of many farmers who work alone and spend many hours each day away from their loved ones. They speak of the loneliness that they feel as they struggle to make a living. They say that bad weather reduces harvest yields, milk production and may even cause sheep and lambs to die in the fields. These factors impact on their income and can be a source of great stress for the farmer and his family.

Poor infrastructure, a lack of public transport and financial constraints all contribute to a sense of rural isolation, which can lead to deep loneliness. They speak of the changing farming legislation that places extra pressures on them and they often feel that they have no one who really understands the stress that they endure. Some admit to depression or acknowledge an unhealthy dependence on alcohol or other substances to relieve the ache in their hearts. Fearful of being seen as 'weak' some are reluctant to seek medical help as they fear hospitalisation and they may have no one to carry on the daily care of livestock and crops.

Taking the first step to reach out for support can be difficult. Fortunately today, there is a greater awareness of the mental health needs of the farming community. Farming organisations reach out and provide mental health awareness workshops to rural communities encouraging them not to be afraid to acknowledge their need for help early in their struggle. Much can be done to support people to regain their self-confidence, self-esteem and to overcome their difficulties. They are then able to raise awareness of the needs of others and to support them on their journey to wellness.

The natural beauty of the countryside can be a soothing balm to a weary heart but nothing supersedes human companionship. We all need people who really listen to us, especially at times when we may be struggling with an issue. Jesus offers words of comfort to all who suffer when he invites them to rest in him.

Come to Me, all who are weary and heavy-laden, and I will give you rest. (Mt 11:28)

THOUGHT TO TAKE AWAY

May we be forever grateful for all who till and care for the earth and for the fruits that it bears us.

REFLECTION 17: SURGEONS

Those who are well have no need of a physician, but those who are sick. (Lk 5:31)

Each day, many thousands of people undergo surgical procedures in hospitals. The gift that surgery bestows on society cannot be over-emphasised as universal access to safe, affordable surgical and anesthesia care when needed saves lives, prevents disability and promotes economic growth.

> *My flesh and my heart may fail,*
> *but God is the strength of my heart*
> *and my portion forever.* (Ps 73:26)

Wherever possible, hospital medical teams work together and discuss the condition of their patients before a decision to proceed to surgery is made. This mutual support helps to reassure the patient that the best ethical and medical decisions are made to aid healing. It reduces the feelings of isolation that a surgeon can feel before life-saving surgery is undertaken. Highly trained and professionally accountable, the surgeon is aware that the actions taken may bring great healing or the patient may die on the operating table. Because of this surgeons sometimes speak of the sense of loneliness and isolation that they can feel as they approach the very ill patient. At each stage of the operation, they have to make decisions about a fellow human being who is in a state of great vulnerability.

At the end of the procedure, the surgeon thanks the colleagues who have been a source of support through the operation.

They have reassured the surgeon that good teamwork serves the common good and builds up each person, confirming the idea expressed in John Donne's poem, 'Meditation XVII' 'no man is an island'. We are all interdependent on each other. As they leave the operating theatre, the surgeon reflects on the words of St Paul, 'And whatever you do in word or deed, do everything in the name of the Lord Jesus, giving thanks to God the Father through him' (Col 3:17)

THOUGHT TO TAKE AWAY

Medical ethic committees are faced with a growing number of challenging issues today. Use your voice to ensure that Gospel values are upheld.

REFLECTION 18: PEOPLE IN HIGH OFFICE

I am not able to carry all these people alone, for they are too heavy for me. (Nb 11:14)

This may well be the cry of many government and Church leaders across the world as people look to them for answers to complex ethical and political questions. Strains of the same lament may be heard from the lips of business and charity organisations as they attempt to respond to the cries of the many people who approach them for jobs, higher wages and support with their day-to-day living.

The world is struggling with ecological and moral dilemmas never known before. A sense of overwhelming responsibility to guide all nations to peaceful and fruitful living may rest deep in the hearts of conscientious world leaders. As they struggle to come up with responsible solutions to seemingly impossible situations, their personal sense of isolation and loneliness can be great. We are called to echo the prayer of Timothy as he prays:

I urge that supplications, prayers, intercessions, and thanksgiving should be made for everyone, for kings and all who are in high positions, so that we may lead a quiet and peacable life in all godliness and dignity. This is right and acceptable in the sight of God our Saviour, who desires everyone to be saved and to come to the knowledge of the truth. (1 Tm 2:1–5)

THOUGHT TO TAKE AWAY

What are some of the practical and spiritual ways in which your parish community may support your local Church and government leaders?

REFLECTION 19: NIGHT WORKERS

Come bless the Lord, all you servants of the Lord,
who stand by night in the house of the Lord!
Lift up your hands to the holy place,
and bless the Lord.' (Ps 134:1–2)

The smooth running of a national economy and the safety and wellbeing of its people requires many people to work through the night. Parents are unsung heroes as they care for and support their little children; many hours are spent feeding new babies or caring for a sick child or frail elderly parent as the world sleeps. In so doing, they clearly bless the Lord through the night. These roles are essential but the person may feel lonely and isolated as daylight fades away and the shadows of darkness descend upon the earth.

Family relationships can be placed under strain when the night worker leaves home in the evening and is not able to be present when children gather to do their homework or get ready for bed. A spouse may feel lonely when their partner is not at home or to receive comfort at the end of a difficult day.

Night work can place extra stress on the health of the person as natural body rhythms are disturbed – poor sleep and disturbed eating patterns can lead to an increase in weight, alcohol consumption, depression and social isolation. Greater family communication is needed to address these matters and reduce obvious and hidden risks to the wellbeing of the whole family.

At times the important contribution that night workers offer to society can be overlooked but it cannot be overemphasised; if no paramedics responded to emergency calls many victims of accidents may not survive. An absence of night midwives would jeopardise the health and wellbeing of mother and child as most babies are born at night; many people return home to God in death in the small hours of the morning. The heroic work of the fire service was clearly demonstrated in London in June 2017 when the Grenfell Tower disaster took place during the night. The absence of the fire and paramedic services would have led to an even higher loss of life than that which took place. The immediate compassionate response of local volunteers helped to ease the grief and trauma of victims and their families as people of all faiths gathered to support all who were in terrible distress in the dead of night.

It is comforting to know that God always sees and blesses the work and prayer of all who work and pray through the night – in him there is no darkness and he repays all for their good deeds by day and by night.

Early in the morning, he came walking towards them. But when the disciples saw him walking on the lake, they were terrified saying, 'It is a ghost!' And they cried out in fear. But immediately Jesus spoke to them and said, 'Take heart, it is I, do not be afraid.' (Mt 14:25–27)

THOUGHT TO TAKE AWAY

If you are unable to sleep, pray for all who work or travel through the night.

REFLECTION 20: PEACEKEEPING TROOPS

The cords of death encompassed me;
the torrents of perdition assailed me;
the cords of Sheol entangled me;
the snares of death confronted me.
In my distress I called upon the Lord;
to my God I cried for help.
From his temple he heard my voice,
and my cry to him reached his ears. (Ps 18:4–6)

My life-time ambition was to follow in my father and grandfather's steps and join the army. I signed up when I was eighteen years old. I had heard about 'the war' from my earliest years – thousands of brave men and women had laid down their lives for their country, many paying the ultimate price for peace.

Captivated by the noble graciousness of the war veterans at the Remembrance Day Services, I decided that I too would do my bit for peace. I joined the army to become 'a peace-keeper'.

After years of rigorous training, I was deployed to a war torn country. Nothing had prepared me for the constant noise of battle: gunfire, shelling, intense heat and dust. My youthful enthusiasm was replaced by intense fear. My colleagues' lives were being poured out before me and I was bereft. I imagined my mother weeping as I lay dying many miles from home. Who would bear the message to her and comfort her when the child of her womb was laid in a tomb? (Lk 23:53).

My soul was ripped apart with the image of what could be but I had to stay faithful to my call – God had called me to be a peacemaker and I had to be faithful (Mt 5:9). As I led my troop across the battlefield, I was reminded of the prayer of Micah (Mi 6:8) that I too had to act with justice and walk humbly with my God in our efforts to restore peace. I was to uphold God's law of love and not commit murder (Ex 20:13). I struggled with this overwhelming dilemma. I am a soldier, trained to kill. What was I to do? I prayed as I had never prayed before:

Make me know your ways, O Lord;
teach me your paths
Lead me in your truth and teach me,
for you are the God of my salvation;
for you I wait all day long. (Ps 25:4)

The love of our brother and sister soldiers carried us through. We supported each other through the darkest days and loneliest nights as we grieved for all who had lost their lives. We wept tears of gratitude when God brought us home safely. Our parents were entrusted to us so that we would care for them until God called them home to himself (Jn 19:27).

THOUGHT TO TAKE AWAY

May the courage of all peacekeepers not fail – may their families be comforted as they await their return from the battlefield.

REFLECTION 21: MEDICAL RESEARCH SCIENTISTS

Ah, Lord God! It is you who have made the heavens and the earth by your great power and by your outstretched arm! Nothing is too hard for you (Jer 32:17)

The contribution that medical research scientists offer to society cannot be overemphasised. We rejoice and give thanks to God for the many wonderful breakthroughs that have been made in the treatment of illness. Thousands of lives have been saved by the vision of Alexander Fleming who discovered Penicillin in 1928.

Scientists continue to spend many years in medical laboratories attempting to find a cure for 'an incurable illness'. This is slow, lonely, painstaking work.

Financial implications, government policies and ethical considerations have to be considered before new medications can be developed or released for prescription. Medical research scientists are obliged to uphold their code of ethics. No treatment may compromise God's commandment to uphold the sanctity of human life.

Meanwhile, the ill person and their family await a cure. Their loneliness can be profound as they may feel that they are 'living with a death sentence' and may feel forgotten by medical, pharmaceutical services and the world at large. However, they wish to keep hope alive and pray that one day a new treatment will be discovered that will alleviate their pain or distress.

As a Christian community we pray that the courage of the

sick may not fail; may they know the compassion of Christ with them on their journey. May the Holy Spirit enlighten those whom God has gifted with the great intelligence that is needed to complete this life saving work. In due course, may all join together and ring out their praise to God, 'Sing to him, sing praises to him; tell of all his wondrous works!' (Ps 105:2).

THOUGHT TO TAKE AWAY

A partnership of faith and science improve the quality of life of the sick. May ethical guidelines and gospel values be upheld as scientific advances are made.

REFLECTION 22: MISSING CHILDREN

Thus says the Lord:
A voice is heard in Ramah, lamentations and bitter
  weeping.
Rachel is weeping for her children;
she refuses to be comforted for her children
because they are no more. (Jer 31:15)

The International Centre for Missing & Exploited Children works in conjunction with the Global Missing Children's Network to raise awareness of the issues faced by abducted and abused children. Each year on 25 May the Global Missing Children's Network members pay respect to International Missing Children's Day, honouring missing and abducted children while celebrating those who have been recovered.

I recently spoke to a mother whose son, Tom, had vanished on a day trip to the zoo. She spoke of his great excitement as his twelfth birthday approached. The previous couple of years had been difficult for the family. His beloved grandmother had become very ill and died unexpectedly. Dad had lost his job and the family had suffered financial pressures. The young boy, disillusioned and hurt, had begun to act out. For a long time no one could reach into his aching spirit. His grades had fallen and he had become isolated from family and friends. His parents were frantic with worry, fearing that they 'had lost their son'. Both he and they suffered a profound sense of loneliness and each wondered when 'life would return to normal'. Fortunately for them, a new teacher recognised Tom's anguish and reached out to him. Through the prayers of his parents and the sensitive response of this teacher, Tom's self-confidence and self-belief began to be restored. His behaviour improved, reverting back to its previous well-mannered attitude; he applied himself to his studies, and completed his chores without grumbling. As his twelfth birthday approached, his mother promised to take him to the zoo to celebrate all that was good in their lives.

The night before his birthday, Tom barely slept; he arose at the crack of dawn and donned in his favourite outfit. Overcome with excitement, he barely touched his breakfast. Holding his birthday money and dreams close to his heart he scrambled into the family car. What was delaying mom and dad? Animals, birds, reptiles and fish awaited!

Every new encounter with creation filled him with joy and delight. All was perfect until that awful moment. The little boy wandered off to explore and vanished. It was all over in a few seconds. Cries of desperation rang out as mom, dad and zoo-keepers searched frantically for 'a missing child'. Their anxiety echoed that of Mary and Joseph when Jesus was lost in Jerusalem (Lk 2: 43–45). They returned to the child's favourite animal cages – maybe he had just gone back for one more look?

Other parents joined in the search, holding onto their own children's hands as they did so. Police checked CCTV cameras. The little boy was nowhere to be seen. Social Media, TV and Radio appeals bore no fruit. Volunteers joined in the search combing every inch of the grounds and local area. For three whole days and nights, parents, brothers and sisters cried out to God for the return of the little boy. They had never known such crushing loneliness. They pleaded with God as they had never done before never losing faith in his mercy and love. They knew that they could never live without their little boy. 'The Lord is near to the broken hearted and saves the crushed in spirit' (Ps 34:18).

Oh so suddenly, the miracle happened. Tom had been found asleep in a disused carpenter's shed several miles away. He was unharmed. Their anguish and deep searching loneliness was overcome with joy and gratitude and they welcomed him home. Later, they shared what the experience had been like for each one of them. Their love for each other grew and deepened through this time of great trial. They prayed each night for all parents who have lost a child or for families where a family member has vanished without trace. They promised to raise awareness of the anguish that is suffered by people who vanish and the grief, loss and loneliness that is suffered by their families.

O give thanks to the Lord, call on his name,
make known his deeds among peoples.
Sing to him, sing praise to him;
tell of his wonderful works. (Ps 105:1–2)

THOUGHT TO TAKE AWAY

Pray for all the missing children of the world who have no voice and who are never re-united with their loved ones.

REFLECTION 23: MODERN DAY SLAVES

Oppressing the poor in order to enrich oneself, and giving to the rich, will lead only to loss. (Pr 22:16)

One of the greatest tragedies and social sins of our world today is human trafficking. Men, women and children are trafficked across the world to be condemned to a life of misery and degradation.

The isolation, fear and humiliation suffered by these innocent people is beyond comprehension. Their human rights are exploited by people who ruthlessly strip them of all dignity and use them to meet their own selfish needs. They have been brought into the country under false pretences; the promise of 'a brighter future', security, good living conditions and the promise of being able to support struggling families at home traps the most vulnerable into a social and psychological prison from which it is almost impossible to escape. Passports are confiscated and the victims are forced to live in the most inhumane conditions, working extremely long hours for a pittance of a wage, malnourished and at risk of all forms of violence.

These actions contravene basic human rights. Anti-slavery legislation and good government policies attempt to address these ills but much more needs to be done so that the human rights of all are upheld. Employers are reminded about their obligation to respect all in their employment.

Stop threatening them, for you know that both of you have the

same Master in heaven, and with him there is no partiality.
(Ep 6:9)

THOUGHT TO TAKE AWAY
Trafficked people may be living next door to you or working beside you. What can you do to help them?

REFLECTION 24: THE HOMELESS

Wealth brings many friends,
but the poor are left friendless. (Pr 19:4)

In the winter, when evenings are drawing in and temperatures are falling. I look forward to returning home in the evening to a warm meal, companionship of loved ones and a bed for the night. Sadly, this is not the reality for the thousands who are homeless in our world today.

As a volunteer in shelters for the homeless, I have witnessed grave human suffering as people share a little of their own unique story. They may speak of the breakdown of a relationship, loss of job or poor mental health. Each story is enfolded in a web of loneliness as people speak of the loss of loved ones, the struggles of every day as they try to find food, toilets or a safe place to spend the night. Heart shattering loneliness is the norm as they feel that nobody understands their story but judges them as 'drop outs' or irresponsible members of society. Some speak of their shame as they recount their dependence on alcohol or drugs to help relieve the aching sadness that has taken root in their hearts. Sadly too, thousands of children are affected and may suffer very severe long-term physical and emotional consequences. Education is disrupted or terminated, peer friendships break down and self-esteem is crushed. Young people are particularly vulnerable as they are at risk of all forms of exploitation as they may not yet have developed some basic psychological coping strategies for dealing with major trauma.

Church and state have a responsibility to work together to reduce this awful human suffering in our society. Organisations can respond by: offering a safe place to stay in a crisis, helping homeless people to take the step from homelessness into stable housing, and providing specialist long-term support to help get lives back on track.

Compassionate collaboration between all members of society will help to relief the loneliness of the homeless and in so doing help to bring about the reign of a God who had nowhere to lay his head.

And Jesus said to him, 'Foxes have holes, and birds of the air have nests, but the Son of man has nowhere to lay his head.' (Lk 9:58)

THOUGHT TO TAKE AWAY
The number of people at risk of homelessness is rising. Charities run campaigns to raise awareness and necessary funds to support the most vulnerable. Why not sign up today?

REFLECTION 25: VICTIMS OF NATURAL DISASTERS

The Lord sits enthroned over the flood;
the Lord sits enthroned forever.
May the Lord give strength to His people!
May the Lord bless his people with peace. (Ps 29:10–11)

International news media abound with stories of great human suffering caused by earthquakes, tornadoes, tsunamis and major hurricanes. Climate change and the indifference of some of some of us to the beauty of creation are partly responsible for the suffering of the innocent. We witness images of rising flood waters flash across our TV screens as the homes of the poor are washed away. All too often, thousands of lives are lost as victims are trapped in the eye of the storm and have nowhere to hide from the ravages of nature.

Families are separated from each other; many are lost and human lives are broken and at risk of despair. The scale of this human suffering cannot be imagined. Deeply traumatised, lonely human hearts plead for mercy. They cry out, 'why has this happened to us, we are always the victims of these terrible disasters. We feel abandoned by wealthier nations and governments. We have no insurance to rebuild our homes or our lives. Our life-stock are suffering greatly, our lives are shattered and we feel that nobody cares. It is so difficult to keep faith and to start all over again.'

The voice of the Holy Spirit impels a humanitarian response. Governments, NGOs and aid agencies reach out to relieve the plight of those who suffer. We are challenged to take responsibility for climate change so that the frequency and ferocity of these disasters are reduced. Long-term solutions need to be found so that the lives of those most at risk are not put in danger and that the heart wrenching loneliness caused of major loss is not inflicted upon them any longer.

I establish my covenant with you, that never again shall all flesh be cut off by the waters of a flood, and never again shall there be a flood to destroy the earth. (Gn 9:11)

THOUGHT TO TAKE AWAY

Climate change impacts on our environment. We are co-creators with God and responsible for the protection of our planet for this and all future generations.